Fables & Folktales

Anansi

by Tyler Gieseke

Dash!
LEVELED READERS
An Imprint of Abdo Zoom • abdobooks.com

Level 1 – Beginning
Short and simple sentences with familiar words or patterns for children who are beginning to understand how letters and sounds go together.

Level 2 – Emerging
Longer words and sentences with more complex language patterns for readers who are practicing common words and letter sounds.

Level 3 – Transitional
More developed language and vocabulary for readers who are becoming more independent.

abdobooks.com

Published by Abdo Zoom, a division of ABDO, PO Box 398166, Minneapolis, Minnesota 55439.

Printed in the United States of America, North Mankato, Minnesota.
102025
012026

Photo Credits: ABDO, AdobeStock, Artistly, Getty Images, Shutterstock
Production Contributors: Jennie Forsberg, Grace Hansen, Tyler Gieseke
Design Contributors: Candice Keimig, Neil Klinepier, Colleen McLaren

Library of Congress Control Number: 2025936764

Publisher's Cataloging in Publication Data

Names: Gieseke, Tyler, author.
Title: Anansi / by Tyler Gieseke
Description: Minneapolis, Minnesota : Abdo Zoom, 2026 | Series: Fables & folktales | Includes online resources and index.
Identifiers: ISBN 9798384940012 (lib. bdg.) | ISBN 9798384940777 (ebook) | ISBN 9798384941156 (read-to-me ebook)
Subjects: LCSH: Anansi (Legendary character)--Legends--Juvenile literature. | Folk literature, African--Juvenile literature. | Spiders--Folklore--Juvenile literature. | Gods, African--Juvenile literature. | Tricksters--Juvenile literature. | Conduct of life--Juvenile literature. | Character development--Juvenile literature. | Mythology--Juvenile literature. | Folktales--Juvenile literature.
Classification: DDC 398.2 [E]--dc23

Table of Contents

Fables & Folktales

Fables and folktales are both kinds of stories. Fables are usually short. They teach a clear **lesson**. They often include talking animals.

Folktales are **traditional** stories that come from a group of people. Adults often pass down these stories to children.

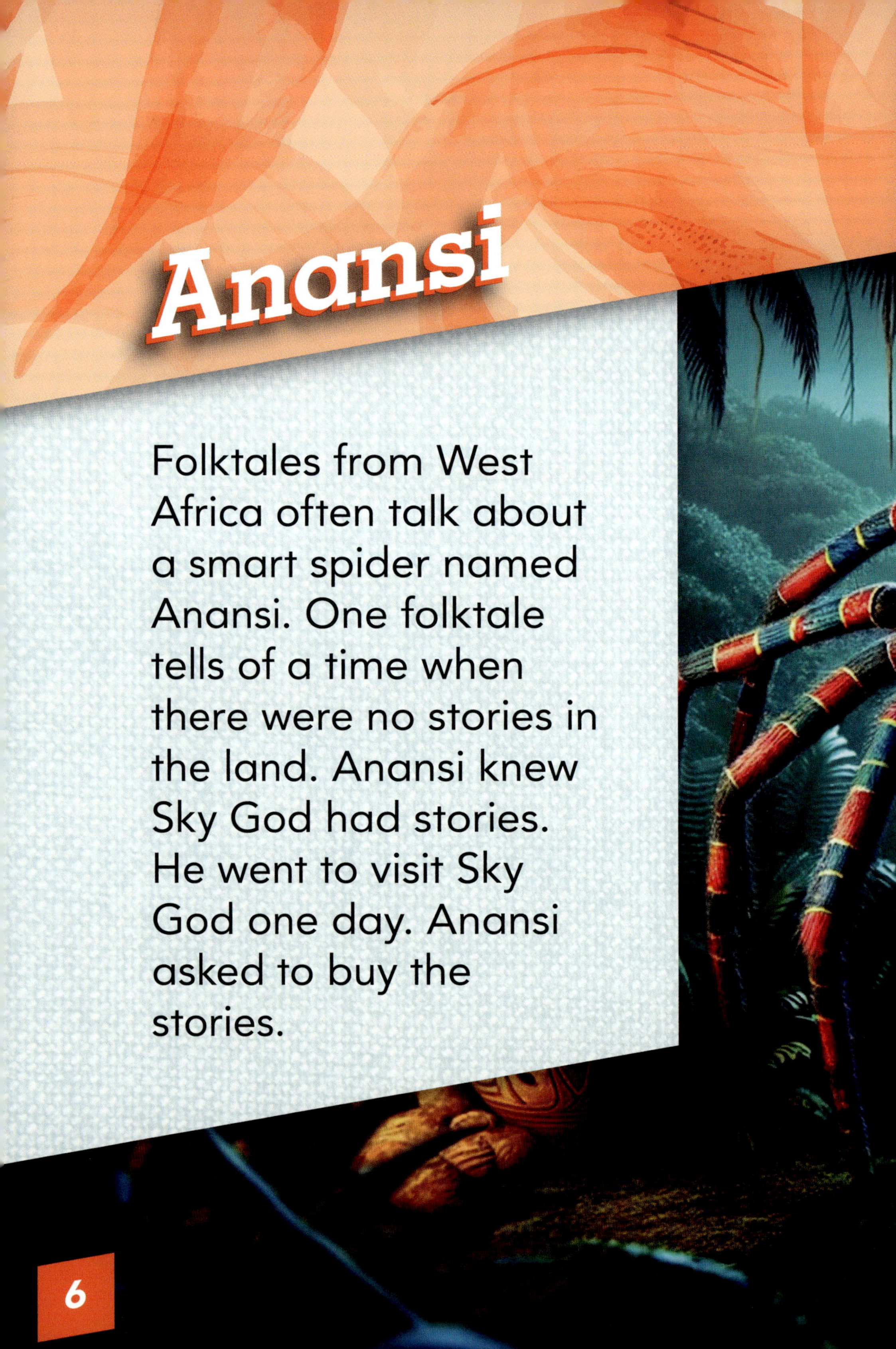

Anansi

Folktales from West Africa often talk about a smart spider named Anansi. One folktale tells of a time when there were no stories in the land. Anansi knew Sky God had stories. He went to visit Sky God one day. Anansi asked to buy the stories.

Sky God did not want to give up his stories, even for money. He said Anansi first had to catch a leopard, a hornet, a fairy, and a snake. After that, Anansi could have Sky God's stories. To succeed, Anansi would need to use his wits.

First, Anansi dug a hole so a leopard would fall inside it. He offered to help the leopard out of the hole using his spider's web. The leopard became trapped in the web!

Next, Anansi went to a hornet's nest. He spilled water over the nest to pretend it was raining. He **convinced** a hornet to hide from the rain inside an empty **gourd**. Anansi shut the gourd.

To catch a fairy, Anansi put sticky sap on a doll and set it near some yams. A fairy ate the yams and thanked the doll. When the doll didn't reply, the fairy slapped her and stuck to the sap.

Finally, Anansi **convinced** a snake to lie down next to a branch so he could measure it. He quickly tied up the snake. Sky God was **impressed** with Anansi and gave him all the stories.

Lessons

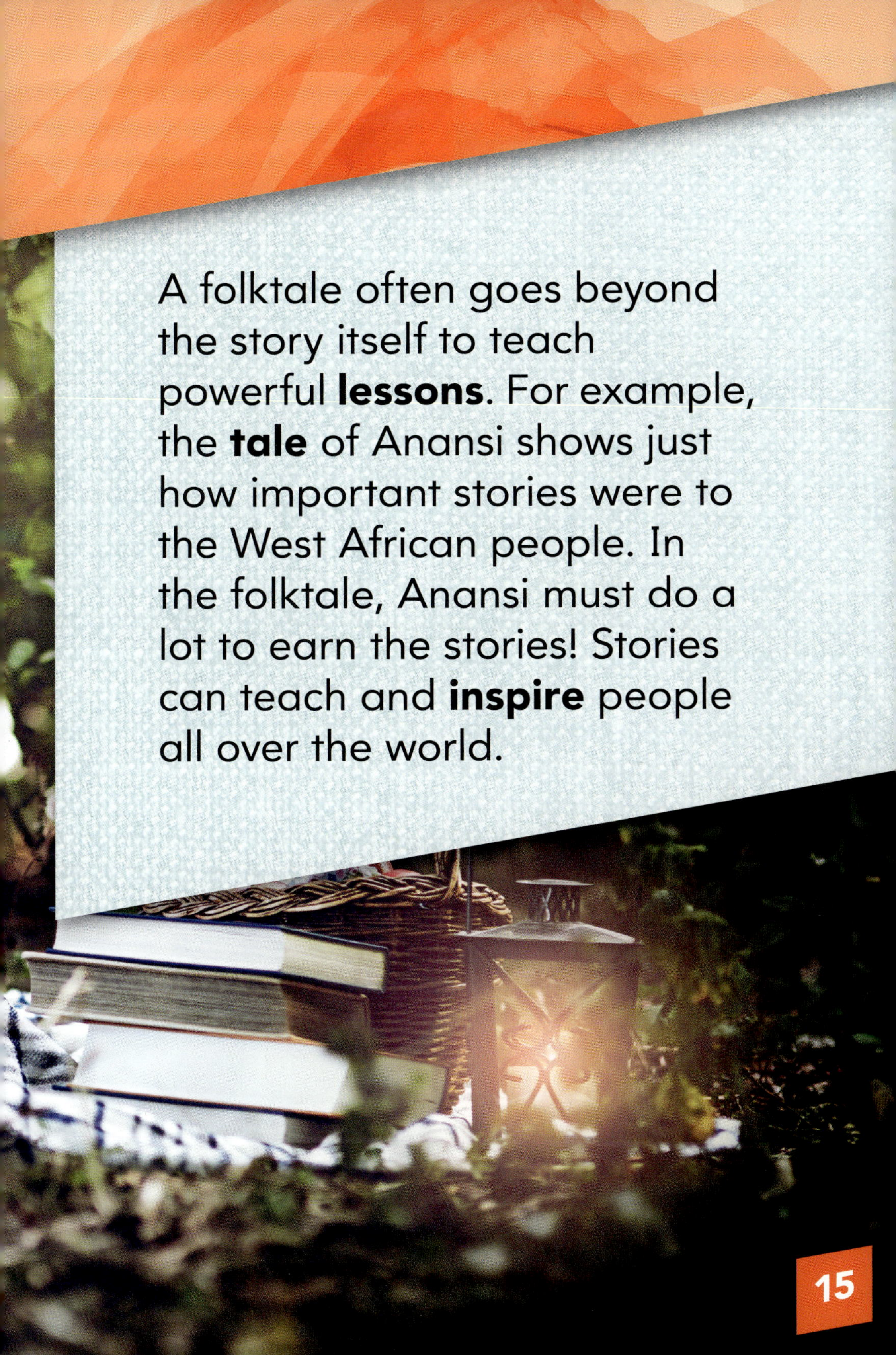

A folktale often goes beyond the story itself to teach powerful **lessons**. For example, the **tale** of Anansi shows just how important stories were to the West African people. In the folktale, Anansi must do a lot to earn the stories! Stories can teach and **inspire** people all over the world.

Stories about how the world was made help people understand their place in it. Stories can teach important **lessons** about how people should act. And stories are fun to hear and tell!

The use of smarts is also important in the Anansi folktale. Without his wits and tricks, Anansi the spider would be too small to trap the four creatures in the story. Being smart about how things are done can help accomplish great things.

For example, **convincing** others to believe in something can require smarts. Doing well in school and at work uses wit too. Before giving up on anything, remember to think about it like Anansi would. What else can your smarts come up with?

More Facts

- The story of Anansi the smart spider comes from the Ashanti people of the West African country of Ghana.
- Now, Anansi is popular in Africa and many countries in the Caribbean Sea.
- In some stories, Anansi the spider can change his shape. He might even look like a human.
- Some stories say Anansi created the sun, the moon, and the stars!

Glossary

convince – to use words to get another to do or believe something.

gourd – a thick, large fruit with a hard skin.

impress – to make someone think highly of you.

inspire – to encourage people to think and act.

lesson – a teaching, or something learned.

tale – a story.

traditional – describing something done regularly and over time by a group of people.

Index

Online Resources

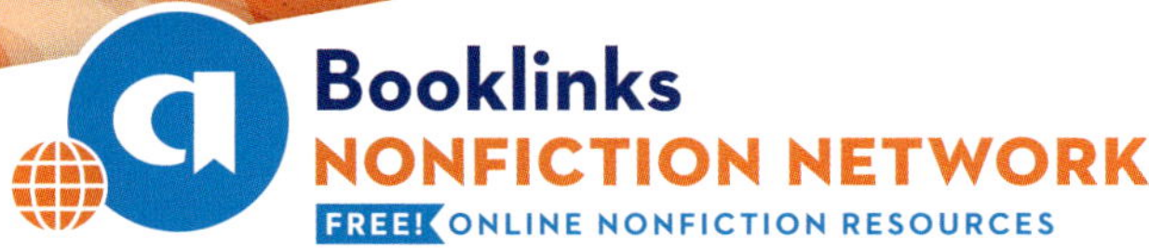

To learn more about *Anansi*, please visit **abdobooklinks.com** or scan this QR code. These links are routinely monitored and updated to provide the most current information available.